MARTIN LUTHER KING

Troll Associates

MARTIN LUTHER KING

by Rae Bains

Illustrated by Hal Frenck

Troll Associates

Library of Congress Cataloging in Publication Data

Bains, Rae.
    Martin Luther King.

    Summary: A biography of a courageous leader in the
civil rights movement who championed nonviolent protest
and "had a dream" of equality for all.
    1. King, Martin Luther—Juvenile literature.
2. Afro-Americans—Biography—Juvenile literature.
3. Baptists—United States—Clergy—Biography—Juvenile
literature.   4. Afro-Americans—Civil rights—Juvenile
literature.   [1. King, Martin Luther.   2. Civil rights
workers.   3. Afro-Americans—Biography]   I. Frenck,
Hal, ill.   II. Title.
E185.97.K5B34   1984   323.4'092'4 [B] [92]   84-2666
    ISBN 0-8167-0160-1 (lib. bdg.)
    ISBN 0-8167-0161-X (pbk.)

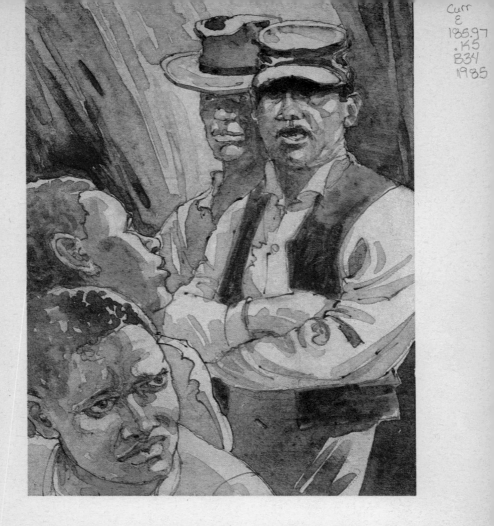

In 1865, the American Civil War ended and the slaves were freed. But life for many black people did not improve very much. The United States Constitution said that all people were equal; yet segregation laws in some states continued to treat blacks unfairly.

In some states, blacks had to attend separate and inferior schools. They were not allowed to vote. They could not use public transportation and facilities on an equal basis with whites. Well into the twentieth century, blacks were denied the rights guaranteed to them in the Constitution.

It was into this world that Martin Luther King, Jr., was born on January 15, 1929. His mother, Alberta, was a schoolteacher, and his father, Martin Luther King, Sr., was a Baptist minister. They lived in Atlanta, Georgia, near the Ebenezer Baptist Church, where Mr. King served as minister. Young Martin's parents were educated, devout, and highly respected members of the community.

In their home, Martin, his sister Christine, and his brother Alfred Daniel, were given a sense of self-worth. Mr. King always told them that they were the equal of anyone. Young Martin believed what his father told them, but the outside world told him something else.

In Atlanta and other parts of the South, blacks were not treated the same as whites. For example, a white person who wanted to ride a bus simply got on, paid the fare, and took a seat. But a black person got on, paid the fare, got off again, walked to the rear door of the bus and got on there. Blacks could only sit in the back of the bus. If all the seats became filled, the blacks had to give up their seats to white people who got on.

All of young Martin's experiences as a black made a permanent impression on him. He was a very bright, quiet, and intense child, with a strong sense of right and wrong. Martin learned to read at an early age, and he read everything he could get his

hands on. His parents encouraged him to learn because they valued education as the key to a worthwhile life.

Martin Luther King, Jr., was an exceptional student from the very beginning. So it came as no surprise when he was accepted by Morehouse College at the age of fifteen. Morehouse, from which his father had graduated, was a college in Atlanta for black men.

While he was at Morehouse, young Martin became interested in religion and philosophy. He began to think of following his father into the ministry. But first, he wanted to get as much education as possible.

After graduating from Morehouse College at the age of nineteen, Martin entered Crozer Theological Seminary, in Chester, Pennsylvania. He was now the Reverend Martin Luther King, Jr., having been ordained a minister when he was eighteen. He was also assistant pastor to his father at the Ebenezer Baptist Church.

It was during his two years at Crozer that Martin began to study the teachings of Henry David Thoreau and Mahatma Gandhi.

Henry David Thoreau was an American writer and philosopher who lived during the nineteenth century. He believed that people should not obey unjust laws. For example, Thoreau refused to pay a church tax imposed by local government in the state of Massachusetts. He did this because the United States Constitution provides for the separation of church and state. Therefore, he said, the tax was unjust, and he would not pay it. For this action, Thoreau was sent to jail, and he went willingly.

Thoreau's form of protest is called passive resistance. It means that, while he would not obey a law he felt was unjust, he would not protest against it in a violent way. Furthermore, Thoreau was willing to accept the punishment that resulted from breaking the law. In this way, he hoped to bring attention to his argument and thereby influence others to change the law.

Mahatma Gandhi was a twentieth-century Indian lawyer, and a religious and political leader. He believed in Thoreau's philosophy of passive resistance and used it to help his people gain independence from Great Britain.

Gandhi and his followers went to jail many times for their nonviolent passive resistance to oppressive British laws. After many years of resistance and jailings, Gandhi's movement won independence for India in 1947.

The concept of passive resistance made a deep impression on Martin Luther King, Jr. Clearly, the discrimination against American blacks was unjust. But the young Baptist minister could not accept the idea of violent protest against this injustice. So he began to think about applying the principles of Thoreau and Gandhi to the cause of his people.

Meanwhile, Martin obtained a master's degree from Crozer. His father hoped the young man would come home now to the Ebenezer Baptist Church. Instead, Martin went to Boston University, to study for his doctorate in philosophy. There, he met and married Coretta Scott, a talented music student at the New England Conservatory. From the very beginning, she shared his beliefs and work in the civil-rights movement.

While he was completing his doctor's degree, King was offered a position as pastor of the Dexter Baptist Church in Montgomery, Alabama. He accepted, and the Kings moved there in September 1954. It was in Montgomery that Martin Luther King, Jr., first put into practice his belief in passive resistance.

The incident that triggered this action occurred in December 1955. Rosa Parks, a black woman, took a seat on a Montgomery bus on her way home from work. The bus soon filled up with passengers, and the driver told Mrs. Parks to give her seat to a white man. Mrs. Parks, very tired from a hard day's work, refused the order.

The bus driver called a police officer, who arrested Mrs. Parks. In reaction to this

incident, the black community staged a one-day boycott of the bus line. That is, no black person would ride the buses on that day.

When Mrs. Parks was brought to trial she was found guilty of violating a Montgomery city ordinance. She had to pay a fine. This led the black community to form a group called the Montgomery Improvement Association. They elected Martin Luther King to lead it.

The group proposed a further boycott of all public transportation in Montgomery. It would last until blacks were given equal treatment on public conveyances. The white community responded with violence. Martin Luther King received death threats. His house was bombed. Blacks were threatened, beaten, and fired from their jobs. But under King's courageous leadership, the nonviolent boycott continued.

Black ministers in other parts of the South, encouraged by the movement in Montgomery, decided to form an organization called the Southern Christian Leadership Conference. Martin Luther King, Jr., was elected its president.

By this time, the United States Supreme Court had overthrown the Montgomery bus ordinance. This decision had far-reaching effects. It meant that public facilities throughout the South would be available to all people on an equal basis. The reaction of white segregationists was more violence.

Martin Luther King, Jr., lived his beliefs. He was jailed many times for disobeying unjust laws. But he continued to preach love and nonviolence. In this way, he inspired the civil-rights movement, and the segregationist structure throughout the nation began to crumble.

In 1963, Dr. King led a march on Washington, D.C. that was attended by more than 200,000 people—both blacks and whites. They listened to a speech in which King said, "I have a dream that one day this nation will rise up and live out the true meaning of its creed, 'we hold these truths to be self-evident; that all men are created equal....'"

These words, blending Dr. King's own eloquence with that of the Declaration of Independence, rang out to the crowd in Washington and to millions more throughout the world. Martin Luther King spoke for everyone who had suffered injustice and who shared his vision of freedom and equality.

The civil-rights movement took more and more of Dr. King's time. It left little time for his position as pastor of the Ebenezer Baptist Church, to which he had succeeded in 1960. There were protests to lead against unequal treatment in housing and restaurants, in voting and education, in employment, and in just about every other aspect of life.

King never stopped working and never lost his faith in nonviolence. For his work and his effect upon the world, Martin Luther King, Jr., was awarded the Nobel Peace Prize in 1964.

Time and again, Dr. King's life and the lives of his wife and four children were threatened. More than once he was physically attacked. Still, nothing could stop him from working toward his dream.

Then, on April 3, 1968, Dr. King went to Memphis, Tennessee, to give support to striking sanitation workers in that city. The next day, as he stood on the balcony of his motel room, talking to his aides, a shot rang out. Dr. King fell, mortally wounded by a rifle bullet fired by James Earl Ray, an escaped convict.

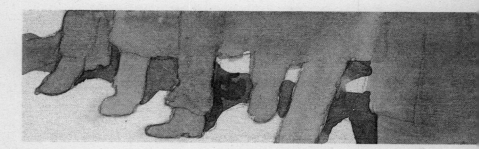

Martin Luther King, Jr., was mourned throughout the nation and around the world. With his death, the civil-rights movement had lost a great leader...a champion of nonviolent protest...a peace-loving man of great vision.

But Dr. King's dream of equality for all lives on.